Starting a Makerspace

WALLINGFORD PUBLIC LIBRARY
200 North Main Street
Wallingford, CT 06492

By Pamela Williams

Published in the United States of America by
Cherry Lake Publishing
Ann Arbor, Michigan
www.cherrylakepublishing.com

Series Adviser: Kristin Fontichiaro
Reading Adviser: Marla Conn, MS, Ed., Literacy specialist,
Read-Ability, Inc.
Photo Credits: Cover and pages 8, 14, 16, and 20 courtesy of
Michigan Makers; pages 4, 6, 10, 12, and 18, Pamela Williams

Library of Congress Cataloging-in-Publication Data
Names: Williams, Pamela, 1965- author.
Title: Starting a makerspace / by Pamela Williams.
Other titles: 21st century skills innovation library. Makers as innovators.
Description: Ann Arbor, Michigan : Cherry Lake Publishing, [2017] | Series: Makers
    as innovators junior | Series: 21st century skills innovation library | Audience: K to
    grade 3.
Identifiers: LCCN 2016032420| ISBN 9781634721929 (lib. bdg.) | ISBN
    9781634723244 (pbk.) | ISBN 9781634722582 (pdf) | ISBN 9781634723909 (ebook)
Subjects: LCSH: Makerspaces—Juvenile literature. | Handicraft—Juvenile literature.
Classification: LCC TS171.57 .W55 2017 | DDC 745.5—dc23LC record available at
    https://lccn.loc.gov/2016032420

Cherry Lake Publishing would like to acknowledge the work of the Partnership for
21st Century Learning. Please visit *www.p21.org* for more information.

Printed in the United States of America
Corporate Graphics

A Note to Adults: Please review the instructions for the activities in this book before allowing children to do them. Be sure to help them with any activities you do not think they can safely complete on their own.

A Note to Kids: Be sure to ask an adult for help with these activities when you need it. Always put your safety first!

Table of Contents

What Is a Maker? 5

What Do Makers Do? 7

How Do Makers Work Together? 9

What Is a Makerspace? 11

What Does a Makerspace Look Like? 13

How to Start a Makerspace 15

What to Put in Your Makerspace 17

Running a Makerspace 19

Inviting Other Makers 21

Glossary 22

Find Out More 23

Index 24

About the Author 24

If you like to tinker, you are a maker!

What Is a Maker?

Have you ever fixed something that was broken? Maybe you changed something that didn't work to make it better. Perhaps you made something totally new that no one had ever seen before. If you have done any of these things, you are a maker!

What Makers Do

A maker is someone who makes things. Makers craft, build, play, and **tinker** with things around them.

Makers use lots of tools and supplies for their projects.

What Do Makers Do?

Makers use materials and tools to create stuff. They may use art supplies, fabric, wood, or power tools. Some use **technology** like computers, machines, or robots. Sometimes makers use a combination of these things in their creations.

A makerspace is a place where makers come to share and learn from each other.

How Do Makers Work Together?

Makers like to share their ideas and projects with other makers. They help each other solve problems that are hard to figure out alone. Sometimes they meet and work in a common place called a makerspace.

Makers help each other with their projects at makerspaces.

What Is a Makerspace?

Have you ever stopped working on a project because you were stuck and didn't know how to finish? What if you had a place to go and get help? A makerspace is a place where makers meet to share materials, tools, and ideas.

Asking Questions

A makerspace is a place to make mistakes and try new things. You can ask other makers questions and get ideas to help you finish your project.

You can build a makerspace anywhere you have extra space.

What Does a Makerspace Look Like?

Every makerspace is different. Makers **design** their spaces to organize all their stuff in one place. A makerspace might contain supplies for arts and crafts. It might also have equipment for cooking or construction projects. It usually has computers and other technology that everyone can share.

Where Are Makerspaces?

Makerspaces can be found in many interesting places. Some have their own buildings. Libraries, schools, and museums often host makerspaces. Others are located in basements, closets, and even garages!

Make sure the space you find for your makerspace has plenty of room for you to work on projects.

How to Start a Makerspace

You can create your own makerspace. First, find a place that is large enough for you and your maker friends to work. Ask an adult to help you find just the right spot. Talk to your friends and family about what you are doing.

Asking for Help

People may be willing to share their **resources** when you let them know about your makerspace plans.

Many makerspaces for kids begin with donated arts and crafts materials.

What to Put in Your Makerspace

Next, make a list of materials and tools you will need to fill your space. Think about things that you already have around you. Scissors, tape, glue, paper, building toys, and recycled materials are all useful in a makerspace. So are screwdrivers, hammers, and computers.

Safety First

Be sure to include safety items such as goggles, table coverings, work aprons, and gloves in your makerspace. Always ask for an adult's help when using glue guns, sharp objects, and other dangerous tools.

Plastic containers are a great way to organize maker supplies. Label the boxes so you can find things quickly.

Running a Makerspace

Organize your maker supplies and label them in containers so you can find them easily. You can hang tools from a pegboard. Keep your tools and supplies neat and clean. After using your space, be sure to put your supplies back in their place. Everyone at the makerspace should pitch in to help clean up.

What will you make in your makerspace?

Inviting Other Makers

Talk to other makers and invite them to join you in your makerspace. Make a poster advertising your space. Post the times your makerspace is open. Finally, go make something in your new makerspace!

Makers Making Together

Every maker has something to offer. Sharing tools, supplies, ideas, and **encouragement** with others will make your makerspace fun and successful.

Glossary

design (di-ZYNE) to plan something that can be made

encouragement (en-KUR-ij-muhnt) words of praise and support that give someone confidence

resources (REE-sors-iz) things that are of value or use

technology (tek-NAH-luh-jee) devices and techniques that do practical things

tinker (TING-kur) to make small adjustments to something in a casual way

Find Out More

Books

Doorley, Rachelle. *Tinkerlab: A Hands-On Guide for Little Inventors*. Boston: Roost Books, 2014.

Fontichiaro, Kristin. *Organizing a MakerFest*. Ann Arbor, MI: Cherry Lake Publishing, 2017.

Web Sites

DIY
https://diy.org
Learn something new from the free video instructions by makers sharing their creations.

National Geographic—Videos
http://kids.nationalgeographic.com/videos
Scroll down to the "Making Stuff" videos to learn how things are made. Maybe you can try to make something you see.

PBS Kids—Design Squad Global
http://pbskids.org/designsquad/
Watch videos highlighting different projects, games, and how-to instructions. Click on Build and try the "Stuff Spinner," which suggests projects using materials you have on hand.

Index

adults, 15, 17
advertising, 21

cleaning up, 19

design, 13

ideas, 9, 11, 21

libraries, 13
locations, 13, 15

makers, 5, 7, 9, 11, 13, 15, 21
materials, 7, 11, 13, 17, 19, 21
mistakes, 11
museums, 13

organization, 13, 19

pegboards, 19
posters, 21
problem-solving, 9, 11
projects, 9, 11, 13

safety, 17
schools, 13
sharing, 9, 11, 13, 15, 21

technology, 7, 13, 17
tools, 7, 11, 13, 17, 19, 21

About the Author

Pamela Williams is a teacher and librarian who uses a glue gun as often as possible. She also loves to upcycle and finds it difficult to throw interesting things away.